# WHEN YOUR PET DIES

Written by
## DIANE POMERANCE, Ph.D.

Illustrated by
## VANESSA MIER

**POLAIRE PUBLICATIONS**
Flower Mound, Texas

Printed in the United States of America
First Printing: 2001


04  03  02  01  010  1 2 3 4 5


Book design by Diane Pomerance, Ph.D.
and Tattersall Publishing, Denton, Texas
Cover and text illustrations by Vanessa Mier


For information, write to:
Polaire Publications
P.O. Box 217
2221 Old Justin Rd.
Flower Mound, Texas 75028


ISBN 0-9708500-0-X

Note: Throughout this book, the author has elected to use the pronoun "he" to represent humans and animals of both sexes.

## DEDICATION

For Katie, Caesar, Spencer & Sophie
my beloved and forever canine
friends, teachers and guides . . .
in gratitude for their shining presence
and spirits, and for the love, joy and
wisdom they have shared with
me along Life's Journey . . .

**D**o not stand at my grave and weep.
I am not there, I do not sleep.
I am a thousand winds that blow,
I am the diamond glints on snow.
I am the sunlight on ripened grain,
I am the gentle autumn's rain.
When you awaken in the morning's hush,
I am the swift uplifting rush
Of quiet birds in circled flight.
I am the stars that shine at night.
Do not stand at my grave and cry . . .
I am not there, I did not die.

— Anonymous

# ACKNOWLEDGEMENTS

I wish to thank my husband, Norman, for sharing so many extraordinary, joyous and cherished animal adventures with me. We have been greatly blessed by and have learned so very, very much from our animal brothers and sisters. I cannot possibly thank Norman enough for his faith in me and for his unwavering encouragement and support of all my endeavors.

Special thanks to the SPCA of Texas for its gracious and generous support in helping me establish its Pet Grief Counseling Program—to Sheila Miller for helping to create and coordinate a strong, ever-expanding and improving program, and to Warren Cox, Lisa Jones, Beth Keithly and Kim Conover for their dedication, hard work and commitment to our program and public education, as well as to the welfare and well-being of both pets and pet owners.

To my parents, Gerda and Benjamin Yapko, I would like to express my love and gratitude for their lifelong support and encouragement. And to my husband's parents, Jean and Joe Pomerance, my love and many, many thanks for their heartfelt and steadfast commitment to and belief in me and my work.

I would also like to thank my dear friends Betty and Chris Christenson for their devoted work in animal rescue and for sharing so many remarkable animals and animal experiences with me. I would particularly like to thank Betty for her kindness, generosity of spirit, unfailing sense of humor, courage and compassion.

**To everything there is a season,**
**A time to every purpose under heaven.**

A time to be born,
    And a time to die;
        A time to plant,
            And a time to pluck what is planted;
    A time to kill,
        And a time to heal;
A time to break down,
    And a time to build up;
        A time to weep,
            And a time to laugh;
        A time to mourn,
            And a time to dance;
    A time to cast away stones,
    And a time to gather stones;
A time to embrace,
    A time to refrain from embracing;
        A time to gain,
            A time to lose;
        A time to keep,
        And a time to throw away;
    A time to tear,
    And a time to sew;
        A time to keep silence,
        And a time to speak;
A time to love,
    A time to hate;
        A time of war,
        A time of peace.

A generation comes, and a generation goes,
    but the earth remains forever.
To everything there is a season,
    And a time to every purpose under heaven.

— Ecclesiastes

**Y**our pet is a very special friend …
one with whom you may share many
great adventures, a lot of fun,
many happy times and
lots of love …

$\mathbf{A}$ pet can be one of many
different kinds of animals;
for example, a bunny rabbit,
turtle, parrot, cockatiel, hamster,
goat, mouse, iguana, llama, horse . . .

or, more commonly, a dog or cat.

**R**egardless of what he is, your pet occupies a
very special place in your heart and life, and fills
you with joy and warmth and tenderness as you
spend time with him.

**Y**our pet is special to you, and you are
special to him.  His eyes may seem to light up
when he sees you—his tail may wag
back and forth enthusiastically,
he may leap happily into your arms,
greet you at the door with a merry bark,
a cheery meow, a tantalizing whistle,
a big wet, slobbery kiss,
a friendly whinny, or simply a loving glance.

**Y**our pet loves you, no matter what, and is your friend forever. No matter how difficult or challenging your life may be, your pet is forever your loyal friend, trusted confidant and a great source of encouragement, love and support.

**W**hen your pet dies, there is a deep void
in your heart and life.

**F**or you and your pet may have been inseparable
… you may have been the best friends ever.

**A**nd then, one day he is no longer there in
his usual spot waiting to play with you. His toys
and treats and feeding bowls or collar and leash
are there, there are photos of you and your pet
on the wall …

**B**ut your dear friend is gone. Gone where, you
wonder? To heaven, with lovely angels to play
with and care for him?

**N**o one you ask seems to know precisely where he may be. But sadness and pain fill your heart and mind; you may feel numb or shocked, you may not be able to pay attention to your friends, brothers or sisters, parents or teachers as well as you did before the death of your pet.

**Y**ou may be angry, frustrated and lonely. You may be overwhelmed by your emotions and feel guilty, hurt and confused all at the same time.

**W**hy did your pet have to die? Couldn't he have lived longer? Didn't you take good enough care of him? Didn't you love him enough?

You may wonder and think about all these things. Will I ever see my friend again? Will we ever play together at some future time? What does it mean to be "dead"? Why do all living things have to die?

You may ask many questions and receive few answers that really satisfy you. You may question your own feelings, for you may feel sadder than ever before ...

... and you may wonder if your feelings are normal.

This little book is written for every child who
has lost a beloved animal companion, and to
each of them we offer this advice:

**W**hen your pet dies, don't be afraid to cry. And don't be shy or embarrassed to show how much you really care. After all, he was your true and special friend—perhaps even your very best or one and only friend.

When your pet dies, it's okay to ask God why or where He has taken your dear companion, and to ask your Mom or Dad or your teacher, minister, priest or rabbi what being "dead" really means and why all living things must die...

You may wish to ask a librarian to recommend books on the subject of pet loss and read them until you find answers to some of your questions.

You may discover that many other children and adults who have lost a pet share many of your feelings. You may also seek help or guidance from a counselor to help you cope with your grief.

You may wonder what purpose your pet's life has served . . .

You may wonder about the meaning
of your own life …

… and if there is life after death, or some very
special time or place when and where you and
your pet may be reunited to share your love
once again.

**W**hen your pet dies, you may cry lots of cries, breathe lots of sighs, feel hurt, grief, guilt, or even relief that he is no longer suffering if he had been sick or injured before he died. You may feel loneliness or emptiness…

…and even frustration or anger. Why couldn't your pet be saved? Why couldn't he live longer? Why couldn't your parents do more for him? Why couldn't the animal doctor (veterinarian) save him or at least prolong his life for a few more days or months or years?

**I**t is very important that you share and express all of your true feelings to trusted family members or friends. Don't try to hide or ignore how you feel. Most importantly, don't grieve alone. The loss of one you have loved is never easy to bear, but don't feel guilt and don't despair, for your pet will always be there ... somewhere deep within your heart.

**W**hen your pet dies, it is very wise to remember and cherish the happy and special times you spent together ... the fun, the joy, the adventures you had and games you played, the secrets you shared, the love, loyalty and devotion that made your friendship so unique.

**G**ratefully remember your pet as a True Friend and Guide who has lovingly accompanied you along a part of Life's Journey ... and through whom you may have learned some of Life's Great Lessons.

**W**hen your pet dies, you may recognize
the divine spark that resides in him, in us,
and in all living creatures.

**Y**ou may want to acknowledge and memorialize
him by having a service that honors and
commemorates the significance of his life.
You may wish to participate in this "funeral
service" with friends and family members who
share your sorrow and who knew and loved your
pet. You may then want to bury his body in a spot
close to your heart—perhaps a place where you
spent hours happily playing together and sharing
your feelings and dreams, or perhaps you might
want to bury him in a pet cemetery and put a
marker with some special tribute to or message
about him at his gravesite.

**Y**ou may visit him every so often, and bring him flowers or some special treat to honor his life. Between visits, it is a good idea to express your true feelings such as anxiety, depression, loneliness or anger to friends and family members and to let them know how much you loved and miss your pet.

**W**hen your pet dies, you may wish to eulogize, celebrate and commemorate his life and remember the comfort, warmth and happiness he brought you by becoming involved in activities such as writing about him in a journal or writing a song or poem or story about him. You may even wish to dance a special dance for him. You may wish to make a photo album full of pictures that will help you to recall and relive your favorite times and fondest moments together.

Such activities will help you eventually to recover from your grief. Recovery means feeling better. Recovery means that one day you will be able to remember the love and happiness your pet brought you and to speak of your loss without suffering or feeling anger, sadness or pain.

**W**hen your pet dies, try to realize all that you have learned from him. For through his personality and behavior it is likely that he has served as both friend and guide and taught you many things about life.

**P**erhaps you have learned lessons about responsibility and trust—what it feels like to have someone rely and depend upon you. Perhaps you have learned more about the nature of true or unconditional love, or courage, gentleness, loyalty or compassion.

**P**erhaps you have learned through this experience that losses are an inevitable and unavoidable part of all our lives, and that often we become stronger having faced these losses ...

... and perhaps your pet's presence in your life has given you new insight and helped increase your understanding and respect for all creatures with whom we share Mother Earth.

**W**hen your pet dies, don't let others criticize or minimize the feelings of love and affection and regard you had for your pet. For only you, in your heart of hearts, know of the wonderful gifts your friend has brought. Don't let some of the silly or thoughtless things they say upset you, such as "Fido was only an animal," or "You can always get another pet," or "Don't feel bad," or "Just get over it," or "Time will heal all wounds."

**I**t may be difficult for those who have never had a meaningful relationship with an animal to understand how important and unique your pet was. They may not understand that no other animal companion can ever possibly replace him, just as no other human being can ever possibly replace you.

When your pet dies, after some time has passed by, you might try this exercise. Look at life through your pet's eyes. Would he wish for you to be sad and lonely for a long, long time? Would he wish for you to suffer pain and sorrow indefinitely?

Most likely, he would want you always to love and think fondly of him, but he would also wish for you to go on with your life. He would know forever that there is a special place in both your hearts to remember the love and joy you shared.

**H**e would probably want to thank you for giving him a happy life filled with treats, toys, games, adventures, conversations and "alone times" you spent just feeling content and peaceful together.

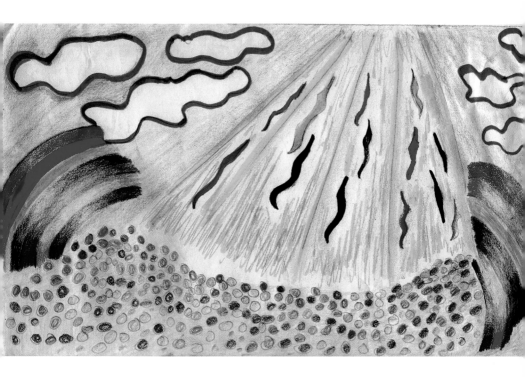

He might also hope that one day, only when you feel ready, that you might open your heart and home to another pet as a loving tribute to him. After all, there are so many animals in need of homes and who are waiting to be adopted by someone who will give them  love and care.

When your pet dies, gently wipe the tears from your eyes and imagine that your friend's spirit soars to the heavens and that his love and devotion fill the skies with a beautiful light that blesses all and symbolizes his existence, gratitude and love for you.

And remember that only you have loved him the way you did … only you will ever know to what extent he enriched and enhanced your life … only you will remember the purity, nobility, and unique beauty of his spirit … only you will cherish in your heart and mind the love you shared with one another …

## THIS LOVE WILL NEVER DIE!

# Words
# of
# Comfort

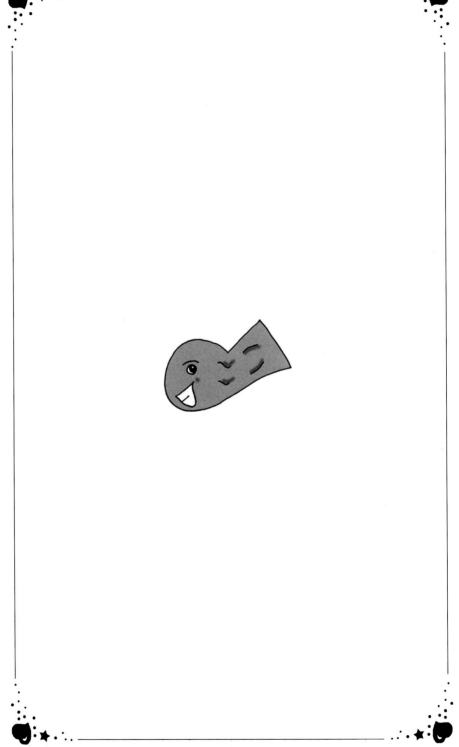

**I** know that whatever God does,
it shall be forever.
Nothing can be added to it,
And nothing can be taken from it.
— Ecclesiastes 3:14


**P**raise the Lord from the heavens,
Praise Him in the heights!
Praise Him, all His angels,
Praise Him, all His hosts!
Praise Him, sun and moon;
Praise Him, all you stars of light!
Praise Him, you heaven of heavens,
And you waters above the heavens!

Let them praise the name of the Lord.
For He commanded and they were created.
He also established them forever and ever;
He made a decree which shall not pass away.
— Psalm 148

There is not a beast on earth,
nor fowl that flieth on two wings,
but they are a people like unto you,
and to God they shall return.
— The Koran


I am the self abiding
  In the heart of all creatures;
I am their beginning,
  their middle and their end.
    Know that my brilliance,
      flaming in the sun,
    in the moon and in fire,
      illumines this whole universe.
        — The Bhagavad-Gita

$\mathbf{A}$pprehend God in all things,
For God is in all things.
Every single creature is full of God
And is a book about God.
Every creature is a word of God.
— Meister Eckhart

**B**e praised, my Lord, for all your creatures.
In the first place for the blessed Brother Sun,
Who gives us the day
and enlightens us through you.
Be praised, my Lord, for Sister Moon and the stars
Formed by you so bright, precious and beautiful.
Be praised, my Lord, for Brother Wind,
And the airy skies, so cloudy and serene ...
Be praised, my Lord, for our sister, Mother Earth,
Who nourishes us and watches us
While bringing forth abundance of fruits
with colored flowers and herbs ...
Be praised, my Lord, for our sister, Bodily Death,
Who no living man can escape.
Praise and bless my Lord.
Render thanks.
Serve God with great humility.

— Saint Francis of Assisi

Thou hast made the moon to measure the year
and taught the sun where to set
When thou makest darkness and it is night.
All the beasts of the forest come forth …
All of them look expectantly to thee
To give them their food at the proper time;
What thou givest them they gather up
When thou openest thy hand, they eat their fill.
When thou hidest thy face, and they are
restless and troubled;
When thou takest away their breath,
they fail and they return to the dust
from which they came;
But when thou breathest into them, they recover;
Thou givest new life to the earth.

— Psalm 104

The insect in the plant, the moth which spends its brief hours of existence hovering about the candle's flame—nay, the life which inhabits a drop of water—is as much an object of God's special providence as is the mightiest monarch on his throne.

— Henry Bergh,
Founder, ASPCA

$T$hen Ezra prayed,

"You alone are God. You have made the skies and the heavens, the earth and the seas, and everything in them. You preserve it all; and all the angels of heaven worship you."

— Nehemiah 9:6

$A$nd God shall wipe away all tears from their eyes; and there shall be no more death, neither sorrow, nor crying, neither shall there be any more pain; for the former things are passed away.

— Revelation 21:4

## About the Author

DIANE POMERANCE received her Ph.D. in Communications from the University of Michigan, Ann Arbor. She has been certified as a Grief Recovery Specialist by the internationally recognized Grief Recovery Institute. She was trained directly by the founder of the Institute, John W. James.

Dr. Pomerance counsels those grieving from any loss; however, she has a special interest in those mourning the loss of a beloved companion animal. The loss of a pet can be devastating to adults as well as children.

Dr. Pomerance is an active volunteer for the SPCA of Texas, K-9 Friends Visiting Therapy Dogs of GTDOG , and the Texas Alaskan Malamute Rescue. She lives in North Texas with her husband and ten canine "kids."

## About the Illustrator

VANESSA MIER was born January 7, 1986 in Fort Worth, Texas. As a small child she showed a great interest in drawing. Her talent flourished in middle school under the tutelage of her art teacher, Mrs. Tallent, who inspired and encouraged her. Ms. Mier intends to go to college, and art work will be her life's focus. "When Your Pet Dies" represents Ms. Mier's first professional work as an artist.

## Order Form

We hope you enjoyed this book from Polaire Publications.

If you would like to order additional copies, please complete this form and send with payment to:

### POLAIRE PUBLICATIONS
P.O. Box 217
2221 Justin Rd.
Flower Mound, Texas 75028
or you may fax your order to: (972) 691-9134

Name _____

Address _____

City, State, Zip _____

_____ No. books ordered  x $9.95   =   $ _____
Shipping & Handling: $3.50 for
    first book,  plus $1.00 for
    each additional book       =   $ _____
            Subtotal      =   $ _____
(Texas residents, please add 7.25% sales tax)  =   $ _____
            TOTAL     =   $ _____

☐ Check: Please make payable to Polaire Publications.
☐ Credit Card:
        ☐ MasterCard   ☐ Visa

Card # _____

        Exp. Date _____

Signature _____

$1 of each copy of this book sold will be donated to: